DREW CALLAHAN

From Struggle to Success: Correcting a Failing Career

Actionable Techniques for Overcoming Setbacks and Thriving in Your Professional Life

Copyright © 2024 by Drew Callahan

All rights reserved. No part of this publication may be reproduced, stored or transmitted in any form or by any means, electronic, mechanical, photocopying, recording, scanning, or otherwise without written permission from the publisher. It is illegal to copy this book, post it to a website, or distribute it by any other means without permission.

First edition

This book was professionally typeset on Reedsy. Find out more at reedsy.com

Contents

1. Introduction — 1
2. Chapter 1: Understanding Your Current Career Situation — 4
   - Section 1: Identifying the Problem — 4
   - Section 2: Confronting Career Myths — 18
   - Section 3: Preparing for Transformation — 21
3. Chapter 2: Building a Foundation for Growth — 26
   - Section 1: Taking Charge of Controllable Skills — 26
   - Section 2: Nurturing Hobbies and Passions — 29
   - Section 3: Emotional Intelligence and Self-Management — 32
4. Chapter 3: Taking Action and Accelerating Growth — 36
   - Section 1: Creating a Personal Growth Plan — 36
   - Section 2: Networking and Building Relationships — 41
   - Section 3: Seizing Opportunities for Career Growth — 43
5. Chapter 4: Sustaining Long-Term Career and Personal Success — 47
   - Section 1: Creating a Continuous Learning Mindset — 47
   - Section 2: Maintaining Work-Life Integration — 50
   - Section 3: Leaving a Legacy — 52

6 Conclusion: 55
7 Resources: 57

1

Introduction

Have you ever felt like you're stuck in your career, like you're doing all the right things, but success still seems just out of reach? If so, you're not alone. Many of us have been in that same place, feeling frustrated, disillusioned, and even helpless. But here's the hard truth that might be difficult to hear at first: you are the common denominator in your story. Yes, you. It's not your boss, your colleagues, or the industry you work in—it's you.

Now, before you close this book, buckle up buttercup and hear me out. Recognizing that you're the one holding yourself back is actually empowering. Why? Because it means you have the ability to adjust course and change the narrative. If you are the problem, then you can be the solution. The first step toward turning your career around is to get out of your own way.

Stop Blaming, Start Taking Ownership

It's easy to blame external factors for your lack of progress. Perhaps you feel overlooked because management doesn't appreciate you, or you're convinced office politics are holding you back. But the longer you point fingers at others, the longer you'll stay stuck. You have to stop blaming your circumstances and start owning your part in the situation.

When we allow ourselves to get caught up in feelings of unfairness, we surrender our power to change anything. The world can be tough, and situations can feel out of your control, but playing the victim only prolongs your frustration. This book is about regaining control and recognizing that your career, and the success you seek, lay firmly in your hands.

Believe in Your Potential—and Take Action

Things begin to shift when you start believing—genuinely believing— you can achieve your goals. Not the unattainable fantasy of overnight success or winning the lottery, but realistic, actionable dreams. The key word here is *actionable*. No amount of wishing, hoping, or waiting is going to change your situation. What will change it is taking deliberate action toward what you want. There is also something to be said for adding spiritual actions.

Achieving success isn't a matter of luck or waiting for the right opportunity. It's about positioning yourself to make those opportunities happen. And that begins with a mindset shift—one where you accept responsibility, stop the self-pity, and start moving forward.

The chapters ahead will give you the tools to make that shift.

INTRODUCTION

Whether you're trying to climb the corporate ladder, switch industries, or find greater personal satisfaction in your work, this book will help you identify practical steps to break free from the patterns holding you back. Remember, you're the common denominator—and that's a good thing. Because if you're the one in your own way, you're also the one who can get out of it and create the success you deserve.

Let's start that journey now.

2

Chapter 1: Understanding Your Current Career Situation

Section 1: Identifying the Problem

Recognizing Career Stagnation

Stagnation in your career often sneaks up on you. Sometimes it's like your shadow, you know it's there but you haven't fully observed or acknowledged it. One day, you realize things haven't changed in a long time, and not for the better. So, how can you tell if you're in a dead-end job?

Signs of a Dead-End Job

Identifying whether you're in a dead-end job is crucial for determining your next steps. Here are the key signs to watch for:

CHAPTER 1: UNDERSTANDING YOUR CURRENT CAREER SITUATION

Lack of Promotions or Advancement Opportunities

One of the clearest signs that your career has hit a dead end is the absence of upward mobility. If you've been in the same role for years without a promotion or significant change in responsibilities, it's a red flag. While some industries or companies may have slower promotion tracks, consistently being overlooked or passed over for new roles could mean that your current environment isn't offering room for growth. If you find that your efforts, achievements, and experience aren't translating into advancement, it's time to reassess whether you're in the right place to thrive. Understand that ideas or proposals you've presented to management for consideration but aren't acted upon are also red flags.

Minimal or No Skill Development

A dead-end job often comes with a lack of opportunities to develop new skills. If you're not learning anything new or challenging yourself, your career is stagnating. Roles that don't push you to grow or provide professional development opportunities—whether through training, mentorship, or new projects—can leave you feeling like you're on autopilot. This lack of skill growth not only stifles your potential but also makes you less competitive in the job market, limiting your future opportunities. Don't be fooled into thinking the company is tracking your progress of the online courses they offer and that they are seriously considering you as a viable candidate. Oftentimes, these trainings are carrots to dangle in front of you.

Repetitive and Unchallenging Work

If your day-to-day tasks have become routine and mind-numbing, it's another sign of stagnation. In a healthy, growing career, you should be taking on new challenges that stretch your abilities and keep you engaged. In a dead-end job, however, your responsibilities remain the same year after year. You stop being challenged, and work starts to feel more like a checklist of mundane tasks than something that excites or inspires you.

Lack of Feedback or Recognition

In a thriving work environment, you should be receiving regular feedback and recognition for your efforts. If your hard work is consistently ignored, or you're not receiving constructive input on how to improve and grow, you might be in a dead-end role. The absence of feedback suggests that your managers or organization may not be invested in your development. It can also indicate that they don't see a future for you in the company, leaving you with little incentive to push for growth.

CHAPTER 1: UNDERSTANDING YOUR CURRENT CAREER SITUATION

No Clear Career Path

In a dead-end job, there's often no clear pathway forward. You might not know what the next step looks like, or worse, there might not be a next step at all. Companies that don't offer a clear career trajectory for employees often signal that growth is limited, and you may find yourself stuck in a position without the opportunity to progress. If you're unsure about where your role can lead or your long-term prospects within the organization, it could be a sign that you've hit a professional ceiling.

High Turnover or Low Morale

A workplace where people are frequently leaving, or where morale is low, can be a warning sign. High turnover often indicates deeper issues within the organization, such as lack of development opportunities, poor leadership, or a toxic work culture. If you're seeing colleagues move on to better opportunities while you remain stuck, it's worth questioning whether you're in the right place for long-term success.

Feeling Disconnected from the Company's Goals

In a dead-end job, you may start to feel disconnected from the company's vision or goals. You might feel like a cog in the machine, with no real connection to the bigger picture. This lack of alignment can make your work feel purposeless, which leads to a lack of motivation and personal fulfillment. Sometimes you may notice that the organization doesn't fulfill its own vision and goals. If you don't see how your efforts contribute to the company's success or growth, it may be time to consider a change.

Stagnant Compensation

Finally, if your pay has remained stagnant for years without any raises or bonuses despite increased experience or contributions, that's a strong sign you've hit a ceiling. Compensation should reflect both your growth and the value you bring to your company. If the financial rewards aren't keeping pace with your experience or industry standards, it's an indicator that the company may not be invested in your long-term success.

Identifying these signs is the first step in recognizing that your current role might be holding you back. A dead-end job doesn't just stall your professional growth; it can also impact your sense of self-worth and happiness. Once you recognize these red flags, you can and must begin taking proactive steps to get your career back on track.

CHAPTER 1: UNDERSTANDING YOUR CURRENT CAREER SITUATION

Emotional Impact of Feeling Stuck

Being stuck can take a huge toll on your emotions. Frustration becomes a constant companion, making you question your worth and your abilities. Over time, this frustration can erode your self-esteem, leaving you feeling powerless in your own career. Sometimes the frustration may seep into your personal life, affecting things at home, creating a cloud of negativity that's hard to shake off.

As the frustration lingers, it often leads to a decline in self-esteem, leading to negative self talk. You may start questioning your abilities or feeling like you're not good enough. This lack of confidence can make it even harder to break free from the cycle, as you begin to doubt whether you're capable of achieving more. The longer you feel stuck, the more powerless and trapped you can feel, which only deepens the emotional toll.

Low self-esteem can also trigger feelings of resentment—toward your job, your colleagues, and even yourself. When you're in this emotional space, it's easy to fall into a victim mentality, where it feels like the world is against you. This mental state can hold you back from taking proactive steps to change your situation, leaving you feeling even more stuck than before.

Recognizing the emotional impact of stagnation is crucial because these feelings can erode your motivation, drive, and overall sense of purpose. To break free, it's important to address not only the external factors of your career but also the internal ones—your mindset, emotional health, and belief in yourself.

Assessing Your Career Trajectory: Practical Steps to Evaluate and Realign Your Path

Evaluating where you are in your career compared to where you want to be is a critical step in overcoming stagnation. By taking a practical and action-focused approach, you can assess your career trajectory and make informed decisions to get back on track. Here's how to do it:

Take a Snapshot of Your Current Position

Start by reflecting on your current role and situation. Ask yourself:

What are my current responsibilities?
Am I learning and developing new skills?
How satisfied am I with my day-to-day work?
How does my compensation compare to industry standards?
Am I where I thought I'd be at this stage in my career?
Does my current career align with morals, values, and passions?

Action Tip: Write down your answers to these questions. This helps manifest a clear picture of your present circumstances, so you can objectively assess your career's state.

CHAPTER 1: UNDERSTANDING YOUR CURRENT CAREER SITUATION

Compare Your Progress to Your Goals

Look back at the goals you set earlier in your life and career. If you don't have clearly defined goals in the past, now is the time to do it. Compare where you are now to where you expected or hoped to be. Don't be afraid to include your dreams for your career and life goals. It's important to include your life goals and dreams because it is likely you achieved a few of those. You need to recognize those wins and be thankful for them. By doing so you are building a positive mindset. If you bought a car, a house, graduated from HS or college, got married, had children, the list goes on, these are great accomplishments to be proud of and prove your worthy to move forward.

Questions to ask:

What were my career expectations when I started in this role? Have I met them?

How much progress have I made toward my long-term career goals?

Am I advancing at a pace I'm happy with?

Action Tip: If you've fallen behind, identify specific reasons why. Is it because of external factors (company structure, job limitations), or internal factors (lack of effort, avoidance of new challenges)?

Identify Gaps Between Your Current Role and Your Future Aspirations

Once you've assessed where you are versus where you want to be, look for the gaps. These gaps could be:

Skill Gaps: Are there skills you need to develop that your current role doesn't offer? Don't forget to include skills for hobbies that could help pivot to entrepreneurship.

Experience Gaps: Are you missing key experiences, such as leadership roles or project management, that are essential for the next step?

Network Gaps: Do you have the right mentors, contacts, or industry connections to move forward?

Action Tip: List these gaps clearly and break them down into manageable pieces. For example, if you need leadership experience, look for opportunities to lead small teams or initiatives in your current role, or seek volunteer leadership opportunities outside of work.

Conduct a Career SWOT Analysis

A SWOT analysis (Strengths, Weaknesses, Opportunities, and Threats) is an effective tool for assessing your career.

Strengths: What are your core competencies and accomplishments? What makes you stand out in your field?

Weaknesses: What skills or experiences are holding you back? Where are your blind spots?

Opportunities: Are there emerging trends or roles in your industry that you can capitalize on? Can you take advantage of any internal opportunities at your current job?

Threats: What external factors might hinder your progress (e.g., industry shifts, layoffs, automation)? Are you at risk of becoming obsolete in any way?

Action Tip: Once you've completed your SWOT analysis, focus on how to leverage your strengths and seize opportunities while addressing your weaknesses and minimizing threats.

Measure Your Skill Growth

Regularly evaluate the skills you've developed and those you still need to acquire. Compare your current skill set with the job descriptions or requirements of the roles you aspire to have.

Action Tip: Identify at least two to three skills that are essential for the next step in your career. Find ways to develop those skills through courses, certifications, stretch assignments, or side projects. Commit to learning something new every quarter. Be sure to include personal development and learning as well. Doing this outside of work while focussing on yourself will lead to better mindsets and possibly improved mental health.

Track Your Accomplishments and Impact

One of the best ways to evaluate your career trajectory is by tracking the results you've achieved. These accomplishments will show how much value you've brought to your organization and help you measure whether you're advancing.

Action Tip: Keep a running document of your key achievements, including metrics such as revenue growth, cost savings, or projects successfully completed. If you are in your early career, it is vital that you do this now and keep supporting documents if you can. This will help you assess your progress and prepare for performance reviews or job applications.

Seek Feedback from Others

Sometimes it's hard to objectively assess your own career. Getting feedback from trusted colleagues, managers, or mentors may provide valuable insights into your strengths, areas for improvement, and opportunities for growth.

Action Tip: Schedule a career development discussion with your manager. Ask for honest feedback about your performance and potential growth opportunities. If possible, seek out a mentor who can offer a broader perspective on your career trajectory.

CHAPTER 1: UNDERSTANDING YOUR CURRENT CAREER SITUATION

Analyze the Company's Growth and Your Role in It

Your career advancement is often tied to the growth and health of your company. Assess whether the organization itself is providing the opportunities you need to succeed.

Questions to ask:

Is the company growing or shrinking?

Are there regular promotions and internal movements?

Does the company invest in employee development (training, leadership programs)?

Action Tip: If your company isn't growing or providing opportunities for advancement, it might be time to explore roles at other organizations where you can grow faster.

Benchmark Yourself Against Peers

Look at how your career progress compares to others in similar roles or industries. This isn't about competition—it's about understanding whether your pace of advancement is on par with industry standards.

Action Tip: Research job descriptions for roles similar to yours to see what qualifications and experiences are expected. Use networking events or professional associations to ask peers about their career paths and progress.

Set New Goals and Create an Action Plan

After completing this assessment, it's time to set new goals and take action. Whether it's improving your skills, seeking new responsibilities, or even considering a job change, create a clear action plan.

Action Tip: Set SMART goals (Specific, Measurable, Achievable, Relevant, Time-bound) for your career. For example, if you want a promotion, a SMART goal might be: "I will gain leadership experience by leading two new projects in the next six months."

Regularly Reassess Your Progress

Career assessments aren't a one-time task. Routinely checking in with yourself ensures that you stay on track and adjust when necessary.

Action Tip: Set aside time every three months to review your progress. Revisit your goals, track your accomplishments, and assess any new gaps or opportunities. Adjust your plan as needed to stay aligned with your long-term objectives. Quarterly reviews allow you more opportunity for course corrections throughout the year.

By taking these practical steps, you'll have a clear and actionable understanding of your career trajectory. This process not only helps you recognize where you are and where you're headed but also gives you the tools to take control of your future and achieve the success you desire.

CHAPTER 1: UNDERSTANDING YOUR CURRENT CAREER SITUATION

Understanding Why You're Stuck

If you're feeling stuck in your career, it's important to recognize both the internal and external factors contributing to your situation. Internal factors, such as personal habits or fear of failure, are within your control. You may be procrastinating, resisting change, or failing to take initiative. External factors, like company culture or lack of growth opportunities, can also limit your progress. Understanding which factors are at play helps you know when to take personal action or consider a change in your work environment. Focus on controlling the controllables.

Complacency plays a significant role in career stagnation. Settling for "good enough" may feel comfortable, but it prevents you from growing. You may avoid challenges, stick to what you know, and stop pushing for advancement. Breaking free from this mindset requires stepping out of your comfort zone and continuously seeking new opportunities to grow. Investing your time in a "Mastermind Group" may also help you sharpen your skills.

Self-awareness is key. Identifying skill gaps and unproductive mindsets is essential to moving forward. If you're missing important skills for your desired role or holding onto negative beliefs that hold you back, it's time to take action. By recognizing these issues and addressing them, you can unlock new potential and move past career stagnation or complacency.

The Cost of Staying Stuck

Remaining in a stagnant career comes at a very significant cost, not just professionally, but personally. Over time, the lack of progress can erode your sense of personal fulfillment. When you feel like you're not growing or achieving your potential, it can create a lingering dissatisfaction that affects your overall happiness and sense of purpose. This lack of fulfillment and satisfaction can weigh heavily on your mind, body, and spirit, making it harder to find meaning in your work and personal life.

Financially, staying stuck leads to salary plateaus and missed opportunities. Without promotions or skill development, your income may stagnate, limiting your financial growth. As others advance, you might find yourself falling behind, not just in terms of salary, but also in benefits and career-enhancing opportunities like bonuses or stock options.

The emotional toll of career stagnation also affects your relationships. Stress and disengagement from work can bleed into your personal life, leading to frustration, burnout, and strained connections with those around you. Whether it's feeling too drained to engage with loved ones or being preoccupied with career dissatisfaction, staying stuck impacts not only your professional life but also your emotional well-being and the quality of your relationships.

Section 2: Confronting Career Myths

CHAPTER 1: UNDERSTANDING YOUR CURRENT CAREER SITUATION

The Myth of the "Perfect Job"

Waiting for the perfect job is a trap that can keep you from making meaningful progress. Many people delay taking action, thinking the right opportunity will eventually come along. In reality, this mindset leads to complacency, as no job will ever be flawless. Every role has its challenges and imperfections, but that doesn't mean it lacks value.

Growth often happens within imperfect roles. It's through navigating difficulties, taking on responsibilities, and learning new skills that you develop professionally. Sometimes you have to take charge, "man up" and seize the day. While these tropes are often used and seem hokey, they have merit at their roots. Action breeds success. Instead of waiting for ideal conditions, focus on how you can improve and grow in your current position.

Reframing your expectations is key to moving forward. Rather than fixating on finding the "perfect" role, shift your focus to continuous progress. Set realistic goals, seek learning opportunities, and look for ways to evolve where you are now. Progress, not perfection, is what leads to long-term success. Failure is also progress. Stop thinking of it as failure and try to view it as a stumbling block to learn from. Try again.

Debunking the "Loyalty Pays Off" Myth

Staying loyal to one company can sometimes hinder your career growth. While loyalty can create job security, it often leads to missed opportunities for advancement, especially if promotions and raises are slow to come. Sticking with a company out of loyalty may keep you in a comfort zone, but it can prevent you from reaching your full potential. Don't let your loyalty delude you into believing you are more valuable to the company versus the results you are actually seeing from being complacent in your current position.

It's essential to strike a balance between commitment and personal career development. While being a dedicated employee is valuable, you need to assess whether your loyalty is limiting your professional growth. If your company isn't offering new challenges, skill development, actively listening or engaging with employee suggestions, or competitive compensation, it may be time to explore other options.

Job mobility can be a powerful tool for career advancement. Changing jobs or companies allows you to gain new experiences, increase your earning potential, and build a more diverse skill set. In today's competitive job market, moving around strategically is often necessary to keep growing and achieving your long-term career goals. Gone are the days of longevity at one corporation. Career-minded individuals simply don't stay that jobs for an average of 5 to 10 years in the current job market.

The Fear of Change

Fear often keeps you stuck in your comfort zone, preventing you from pursuing new opportunities or growth. The uncertainty of change can feel overwhelming, leading you to falling into a dreadful cycle of familiar routines, when they no longer serve your long-term goals. This fear stifles progress, as staying in the same place feels safer than stepping into the unknown. Did you know that the Bible tells its readers to not fear 365 times? That's one time for each day of the year!

"What many don't realize is fear can take on multiple personalities, be in different areas of our livelihood, and cause us to accept certain behaviors or beliefs without realizing we are doing it." -Blair Parke

Overcoming fear requires confronting self-doubt and breaking free from career paralysis. Doubting your abilities or fearing failure can stop you from taking the steps necessary to advance. By challenging doubts and focusing on strengths, you will begin to push past the paralysis and take action.

To embrace change, you need to adopt a mindset that welcomes calculated risks. Instead of fearing change, approach it as an opportunity for growth. Evaluate potential risks, but don't let fear dictate your choices. Creating this mindset empowers you to move forward, learn, and thrive in new situations.

Section 3: Preparing for Transformation

Shifting Your Mindset

One of the most important steps in turning your career around is shifting from a victim mindset to a proactive one. Don't view yourself as powerless in difficult situations, embrace the belief that you can take charge and make things happen. This thought process will encourage you to stop blaming external factors and start looking for solutions.

Reframing challenges as opportunities for growth and learning is another key part of this mental exercise. Every obstacle is a chance to learn and improve. When you start viewing difficulties through this lens, you'll find new ways to grow, rather than feeling defeated by them.

Cultivating resilience and mental toughness is crucial for navigating the peaks and valleys of your career. Building these traits helps you recover from setbacks more quickly, maintain focus on your goals, and stay committed to your path even when things get tough. Resilience allows you to keep moving forward, no matter what challenges you face.

Defining Career Success

Career success begins with defining what it means for you personally. Not what it means to your family and friends, this is your career and you are the one putting in the time and effort. It's not a one-size-fits-all concept. You need to establish your own metrics—whether that's financial stability, career advancement, work-life balance, or making an impact. Knowing what truly matters to you allows you to pursue goals that are meaningful and fulfilling.

Achieving success requires balancing personal fulfillment with professional achievement. While climbing the career ladder is important, it shouldn't come at the expense of your well-being or personal happiness. Success is about finding harmony between these two areas, ensuring that you feel fulfilled in both

CHAPTER 1: UNDERSTANDING YOUR CURRENT CAREER SITUATION

your work and your life outside of it. It's possible this might include making lifestyle changes and financial sacrifices.

Finally, remember that success is a continuous journey. It's not a single milestone, but a process of growth and evolution. As your career and personal life change, your definition of success may shift too. Embrace the journey and keep striving for progress rather than perfection.

Setting a Baseline: Self-Assessment

Before journeying forward, it's vital to evaluate where you stand now. Start by examining both your current skills and emotional health. Understanding your strengths and gaps in knowledge will help you discover where you need to grow, while gaining a clear picture of your emotional state can shed light on how you handle stress, deal with change, and challenges in your career.

Identifying your strengths, weaknesses, and untapped potential is a crucial step. Take an honest look at what you're good at and where you could improve. Often, there are abilities or passions you haven't fully explored yet—recognizing these can unlock new opportunities for growth.

Creating a roadmap for your career involves bridging the gap between where you are now and where you want to be. Start by setting specific, measurable goals. Define what success looks like for you—whether it's a promotion, salary increase, or a industry shift. The key is to make your goals clear and time-bound. For example, you might aim to gain the necessary skills for a senior management role within two years.

Next, identify skill gaps that need addressing. Look at skills you currently have and compare them to skills required for your desired role. Research job descriptions or seek feedback from mentors to uncover areas of improvement. Prioritizing these areas will give you a clearer focus on what to develop, whether through training, mentorship, or gaining hands-on experience.

Breaking down your long-term goal into smaller, manageable steps makes the journey less daunting. Instead of focusing on the end goal alone, start with smaller tasks that build toward it. For example, if your goal is a leadership position, your first step might be to take on more responsibility in a project management role. Small wins help build momentum and keep you motivated. Ever hear of Dave Ramsey's "Debt Snowball"? It's the same concept. Small wins breed success.

It's also important to set deadlines and timelines for each stage of your roadmap. Having specific timeframes ensures you stay focused and accountable. For instance, if you need to develop a certain skill, commit to completing a course or gaining experience by a certain date.

Along the way, leverage your network and seek out mentorship. Mentors and colleagues can provide guidance, support, and advice to help you achieve your goals. Networking can open up new opportunities and offer valuable insights into what it takes to succeed in your chosen field.

Tracking your progress is essential. Your roadmap should be flexible and open to adjustments. Regularly assess how far you've come and be ready to revise your plan if needed. As you encounter challenges or shift your priorities, your roadmap should evolve with you.

Finally, it's important to celebrate achievements, no matter how small. Rewarding progress keeps you motivated and reminds you of how far you've already come. Stay committed to this dynamic approach. Your roadmap will guide you toward continuous growth and help you adapt to challenges or opportunities along the way.

3

Chapter 2: Building a Foundation for Growth

Section 1: Taking Charge of Controllable Skills

Assessing Your Skill Set

In order to move forward in your career, you need to evaluate the skills that lead to promotions and recognition. Key skills like leadership, problem-solving, communication, and adaptability often stand out as essential for career advancement. In addition, relationship building and partnering with others in the workplace is a commodity that decision makers look for when considering a candidate for promotion. Employers value these abilities because they demonstrate your ability to take on more responsibility and achieve results.

Next, consider where you stand in relation to industry expectations. Take a hard look at your current skill set and compare it with the qualifications typically required for the roles you aspire to. What are the areas where you fall short? Identifying these gaps is the primary step toward improvement, whether it involves technical skills, certifications, or developing soft skills like negotiation and time management.

Finally, map your skills to future roles and career paths. Think about where you want to go in your career and what the necessary skills are to get there. By aligning personal development with requirements of desired roles, you'll position yourself for opportunities and create a clearer pathway to growth. This forward-thinking approach ensures that your skill set evolves alongside your ambitions and dreams.

Developing Core Competencies

Building core competencies such as leadership, communication, relationship building, and problem-solving is critical for advancing in your career. These skills not only help you navigate daily challenges but also position you as someone capable of taking on greater responsibilities. Leadership allows you to guide teams effectively and efficiently, communication ensures your ideas are heard and understood, relationship building garners respect and trust, and problem-solving demonstrates your ability to handle complex situations.

Continuous learning plays a vital role in developing these competencies. Certifications, workshops, and further education are all powerful tools for expanding your knowledge and staying competitive in your field. Whether it's mastering new technologies or refining management techniques, investing in your education helps you stay ahead of industry trends.

Soft skills, like emotional intelligence, adaptability, and teamwork, are equally essential. While technical skills get you noticed, it's often your ability to collaborate, build relationships, and manage emotions that propel your long-term success. Developing these competencies is key to thriving in today's work environment.

Adapting to Industry Changes

In today's rapidly changing job market, staying relevant is essential. Industries evolve quickly, and if you don't keep up, you risk being left behind. The key is to continuously adapt by updating your skills and staying informed about shifts in your field and the workplace in general.

Learning new technologies and keeping up with industry trends is crucial for maintaining your competitive edge. This means not only acquiring technical knowledge but also understanding how to apply it in your role. Regularly attending workshops, webinars, and training sessions helps ensure you're up-to-date with the latest tools and strategies.

Anticipating future needs is equally as important. Staying ahead of industry changes and predicting what skills or knowledge will be in demand, can prepare you for tomorrow's challenges today. This forward-thinking approach keeps you flexible and ready to seize opportunities as they arise.

Section 2: Nurturing Hobbies and Passions

Integrating Personal Interests into Your Career

Pursuing your passions alongside work adds immense value to both your personal life and career. When you make time for activities you enjoy, it fuels your creativity and keeps you energized, which can have a positive impact on your professional performance as well.

Aligning hobbies with your career skills can lead to creative solutions in the workplace. Whether it's problem-solving techniques learned from a hobby or new perspectives gained from your passions, integrating these interests often brings fresh ideas that benefit your work.

Turning your passions and hobbies into a side hustle or even a full career pivot requires thoughtful planning and practical steps. First, evaluate the market potential of your passion. Determine whether there's a demand for what you enjoy doing and if it aligns with skills or knowledge you already have. Research the industry, competitors, and customer needs to see if there's a gap you can fill or a unique value you can offer. Don't be afraid to partner with neighbors or friends for advice if they are already in that space.

Once you've validated your idea, start small by testing it as a side hustle. You can begin by dedicating a few hours a week to your new pursuit. This permits you to explore your passion in a low-risk way while still maintaining your main job. At this stage, focus on building a demonstrable portfolio, gaining initial clients or customers, and refining your offerings. Use the feedback you receive to improve and grow.

As your side hustle increases momentum, consider scaling

it upward. Can it develop into a full-time career? This is the point where you assess whether you're ready for a career pivot. Financial stability is extremely important before taking a huge step—ensure you have a solid plan in place, such as savings or other streams of income, to support you during the transition. Additionally, increasing your skills in areas that will help you run and grow your business—such as marketing, finance, or management—will be essential.

By starting small, continuously learning, and building confidence along the way, you can gradually turn your passion into a sustainable side hustle or even a new career path.

Work-Life Balance and Its Impact on Growth

Maintaining a healthy work-life balance is crucial for avoiding burnout, especially when career demands are high. Engaging in hobbies outside of work provides an essential mental break, helping to reduce stress and maintain overall wellness. By dedicating time to activities you enjoy, you can recharge and return to work with more energy and clarity.

Incorporating downtime and creative activities into your routine can significantly boost productivity. One actionable approach is scheduling regular breaks throughout your day. Short, frequent breaks help refresh your mind and prevent burnout. During these breaks, try engaging in a creative activity like drawing, journaling, or even going for a walk, as it stimulates different parts of your brain and encourages

CHAPTER 2: BUILDING A FOUNDATION FOR GROWTH

innovative thinking.

Another idea is to dedicate time to hobbies that involve creativity or problem-solving. Activities like playing an instrument, painting, or cooking can shift your focus away from work, allowing your mind to recharge. This mental reset often leads to increased productivity when you return to your tasks, as your brain has had a chance to rest and process information in the background.

You can also use weekends or downtime to work on personal projects that inspire you. Doing something completely different from your job but still mentally engaging can improve cognitive flexibility, which translates into better problem-solving and creative thinking at work. Whether it's learning a new skill or exploring a passion project, these creative outlets keep your mind sharp and ready to tackle professional challenges with renewed energy and insight.

Leveraging Hobbies for Networking and Opportunities

Your hobbies can be extremely powerful tools for expanding your network. When you participate in activities you enjoy, you are likely to naturally connect with people who share similar interests, and these connections can possibly lead to meaningful professional relationships. Whether it's joining a club, attending events, or engaging in online communities related to your hobbies, these shared interests create a natural way to build rapport and open up networking opportunities.

The power of community in career advancement shouldn't

be overlooked. People you meet through your hobbies can offer support, introduce you to new opportunities, or provide mentorship. These relationships often grow organically, making it easier to collaborate or seek guidance when needed. Being part of a community built around common passions can help you tap into opportunities you might not encounter in your regular professional circles.

Additionally, passion-driven projects can lead to unexpected career opportunities. Whether you're starting a side business, volunteering your skills, or collaborating on creative ventures, these projects often open doors to new industries, clients, or roles. Leveraging your hobbies this way can lead to career growth that aligns with your interests and values.

Section 3: Emotional Intelligence and Self-Management

Managing Stress and Emotional Setbacks

In high-performance environments, stress management is essential for maintaining productivity and well-being, physical and mental. Techniques like mindfulness, deep breathing, and regular physical activity can help reduce stress levels and keep you focused. Setting boundaries, such as taking short breaks and avoiding frequent multitasking, helps in creating a more sustainable work pace, preventing burnout.

Bouncing back from setbacks requires emotional resilience. When faced with challenges, it's important to shift your mindset from dwelling on the problem to finding solutions. Viewing setbacks as opportunities to learn and grow builds resilience, helping you recover faster and come back stronger.

Creating a self-care routine is so very essential for maintaining balance between your personal well-being and professional responsibilities. The key to building an effective and efficient routine is consistency and personalization—what works for one person may not work for another, so it's important to find activities that genuinely help you recharge.

Start by setting aside dedicated time each day or week for self-care, even if it's just 15 minutes. This could be used for meditation, reading, journaling, or a short walk. Regular physical activity is also a powerful stress reliever—whether it's yoga, running, or going to the gym, exercise helps clear your mind, increase mental health, and boost energy levels.

Incorporating moments of mindfulness into your day, such as deep breathing exercises, prayer, or taking a few minutes to focus on the present, can significantly reduce stress and help you stay grounded during busy periods. Additionally, making time for hobbies or creative outlets allows you to step away from work and engage in something that brings joy, helping you mentally reset.

Prioritize sleep, as well. A regular sleep schedule is too often overlooked but is crucial for maintaining emotional balance and peak performance. Finally, set boundaries in your work life, such as disconnecting from emails or work tasks at a certain time each day, to ensure you have time for yourself.

By regularly practicing self-care, you'll be better equipped to handle stress, maintain emotional stability, and achieve a sustainable balance between your personal and professional life.

Building Confidence in Your Capabilities

Conquering imposter syndrome is a crucial first step to elevating confidence. To combat feelings of inadequacy, recognize that self-doubt is common, even among high achievers. A helpful technique is to regularly be thankful for what you have, remind yourself of your achievements and qualifications, and maintain a record of successes as proof of your capabilities. Additionally, challenge negative self-talk by reframing doubts with positive affirmations and focusing on facts rather than feelings. Personally, the author likes to remember these two Scriptures: Colossians 3:23-24 and 1 Corinthians 10:31.

Mentorship plays a key role in reinforcing your confidence. Having someone experienced who believes in you can provide guidance, constructive feedback, and encouragement when you're doubting yourself. A mentor can help you see your strengths more clearly and provide insights that make professional challenges feel more manageable. Positive reinforcement from peers or managers also boosts confidence, therefore, seek feedback and recognize the value you bring to the team.

Celebrating small victories and incremental progress is crucial for sustaining confidence. Every step forward, no matter how small, is a sign of growth. Acknowledge these moments to build momentum and remind yourself that progress is a process, not a single event. Take pride in small accomplishments to fuel long-term self-assurance, this helps appreciate the journey of personal and professional development.

Emotional Control and Decision-Making

Emotions often play a significant role in career decisions, sometimes clouding judgment and leading to choices based on fear, frustration, or excitement rather than rational thinking. Be aware of how your emotions influence decision-making in order to gain control. When you're emotionally charged, you might avoid risks out of fear (Fear Not!) or make impulsive moves driven by frustration. Understanding this dynamic helps you recognize when emotions are steering your decisions and allows you to pause before acting.

To regulate emotions in high-pressure situations, develop tools like deep breathing and other breathing techniques or exercises, mindfulness, and time-outs. When experiencing stress, these techniques help you stay grounded and prevent emotional reactions from overriding logical thinking. For instance, taking a few moments to breathe deeply can calm your nervous system and help you regain focus, making it easier to think clearly.

Making clear, rational decisions during stressful times requires emotional detachment and practice, it won't come overnight. One effective strategy is to step back and assess the situation objectively, weighing the pros and cons of your options. Seek advice from mentors or trusted colleagues to get an outside perspective and ensure you're not letting stress dictate your choices. By controlling your emotions and focusing on the facts, you can make decisions that are aligned with your long-term goals rather than short-term reactions.

4

Chapter 3: Taking Action and Accelerating Growth

Section 1: Creating a Personal Growth Plan

Defining Short and Long-Term Goals

In chapter one, we touched upon the idea of using SMART goals. Here we will dig deeper.

When setting career goals, it's important to use the SMART framework—goals that are Specific, Measurable, Achievable, Relevant, and Time-bound. This approach ensures clarity and direction. Instead of vague ambitions like "I want to be more successful," a SMART goal would be "I want to earn a promotion to a management position within two years by improving my leadership skills and completing relevant certifications." This kind of goal provides a clear path and measurable benchmarks. Physically writing these down with pen and paper, perhaps in a journal can be very inspiring. When you physically write down a goal, you manifest it into physical reality and declare it. You have then put your goals or dreams into the written word. Revisit them often, read them daily, and speak them outloud. This will have a profound effect on your motivation.

Setting SMART career goals—Specific, Measurable, Achievable, Relevant, and Time-bound—provides a structured approach to achieving success. Here's how to apply each element practically:

Specific goals clarify exactly what you want to accomplish. Instead of vague aspirations like "I want a better job," be detailed: "I want to move into a project management role in the tech industry within the next year." The clearer and more granular your goal, the easier it is to map out the steps required to get there. When setting a specific goal, think about the 'who,' 'what,' 'where,' and 'how'—what exactly you want to accomplish, who can help, what resources you need, and how you'll make it happen.

Measurable goals allow you to track your progress and celebrate milestones along the way. If your goal is to earn a promotion, you might measure it by completing professional development courses or taking on new responsibilities at work. Measurable goals should include metrics, like increasing sales by 15% within six months or completing three certifications by the end of the year. Tracking progress not only keeps you motivated but also helps you adjust if you fall behind schedule. Keep these measurements in the same place as where you wrote and declared your goals.

Achievable goals must be realistic and aligned with your current resources and abilities. This doesn't mean you should aim low; rather, your goals should stretch you without being out of reach. If you aim to switch careers entirely, assess what training or experience you need to make that move possible. Break your larger ambition into smaller, attainable tasks, such as taking online courses or attending industry networking events. Focus on progress, not perfection.

Relevant goals ensure that your efforts align with your broader career aspirations and values. Ask yourself, "Does this goal move me toward the career I truly want?" For example, pursuing a certification in a specific software makes sense if it's widely used in your industry, but might be irrelevant if it doesn't align with where you want to go. This step requires honest reflection on what success means to you, personally and professionally.

Time-bound goals include deadlines that give you a sense of urgency and help prioritize your efforts. A goal without a deadline risks being pushed indefinitely. If your long-term goal is to be a team leader, set milestones like "In six months, I will complete a leadership training course" or "Within the next year, I will lead two major projects." These time frames keep you focused and accountable.

By following the SMART framework, you can set clear, actionable goals that guide your career path. Each component helps turn abstract ideas into practical steps, making success more attainable.

How do you eat an elephant? One bite at a time, as the old saying goes. Breaking down large goals into smaller, actionable steps makes them more manageable. For example, if your long-term goal is a leadership role, you might start by developing specific skills like project management or team communication. These smaller steps not only make the process less overwhelming but also provide regular wins to keep you motivated. You gotta' get those wins, so don't give up at the first or third sign of resistance. Just keep going.

Regularly revisiting and revising your goals is essential. Progress isn't always linear, and your circumstances or priorities may shift over time. By reviewing your goals periodically, you can adjust timelines, refine your focus, and ensure your goals remain relevant as you move forward. This adaptability keeps you on track toward meaningful, achievable career growth.

Aligning Goals with Passion and Purpose

When setting career goals, it's essential to ensure they reflect your true desires, not just external pressures or societal expectations. It's easy to be influenced by what others deem successful, but long-term fulfillment comes from pursuing what genuinely excites and motivates you. Reflect on your values, interests, and what you want to contribute to your field, rather than conforming to what others think you should achieve. This can be extremely difficult when family feels they are invested in your success and career. If you have your own family, keep in mind that you need to be responsible for helping to provide.

Balancing passion-driven goals with practical career milestones is crucial. While pursuing what you love is important, it's equally vital to ensure your goals are realistic and aligned with tangible career growth. For example, if your passion is creative writing but you work in marketing, a practical goal might involve using writing skills to create compelling content in your role, while also pursuing side projects that tap into your deeper creative ambitions.

Crafting a mission statement for your career path can provide clarity and direction. A personal mission statement is a concise declaration of your purpose and the impact you want to have in your career. It's equally important to physically write this down, as mentioned previously for goal setting. Writing it down and frequently revisiting your mission statement and reading it aloud helps you stay focused on what truly matters and serves as a guide for making career decisions that align with your long-term vision. Having a clear sense of purpose ensures that each goal you set brings you closer to achieving meaningful success.

Tracking and Measuring Progress

Tracking and measuring progress in your career is crucial for ensuring you're on the right path. Tools like journaling, performance reviews, and personal assessments can help you evaluate your growth. Apps like Trello or Notion can also organize goals and track milestones. Regular self-assessments allow you to measure your skill development, leadership growth, or how much responsibility you've gained over time.

Career advancement isn't just about promotions. Look at other indicators like increased autonomy, new skills, or how often colleagues seek your expertise. These subtle markers of growth highlight your development even if formal titles remain unchanged.

Regular self-reflections are vital for adapting your path. Take time to review your goals every few months (quarterly is a good place to start) to see if you need to adjust based on new opportunities or challenges. This flexibility ensures that you stay aligned with both your evolving career aspirations and the realities of the job market.

Section 2: Networking and Building Relationships

The Power of Networking for Career Success

Networking plays a vital role in career success, opening doors to new opportunities, mentorship, and insights you might not encounter otherwise. Leveraging your professional networks can lead to job referrals, collaborations, and industry advice from seasoned experts. Building relationships with mentors who've walked your path helps you navigate challenges and accelerates your growth.

Expanding your circle beyond your immediate industry is also essential. Cross-industry relationships can offer fresh perspectives, spark innovative ideas, and expose you to different ways of thinking, all of which broaden your professional and personal horizons.

Creating a well-rounded network that supports both your career and personal growth requires intentional effort. Seek out diverse connections—those who inspire you, challenge you, and align with your values. A strong, supportive network can be a key driver in achieving both professional success and personal fulfillment.

LinkedIn is a wonderful place to develop and cultivate a network. It requires plenty of effort and consistency to reach out to strangers and start a professional relationship. The 2-Hour Job Search by Steve Dalton is a fantastic reference for utilizing LinkedIn.

Authentic Relationship-Building

Building genuine connections is about more than just exchanging business cards; it's about forming relationships based on trust and shared interests. Authentic connections grow when you show genuine interest in others, listen actively, and engage in meaningful conversations, rather than focusing solely on what you can gain from the relationship.

Reciprocity is essential in maintaining strong networks. Offering value—whether through advice, support, or connections—makes your relationships mutually beneficial. People are more inclined to help you if they feel valued in return. Always exhibit integrity with network connections and honor your word and commitments.

Long-term relationships thrive on mutual benefits. Consistently check in, offer help when needed, and find ways to contribute to others' success. By prioritizing a relationship's longevity over short-term gains, you create lasting connections that can grow alongside your career.

Networking in a Digital World

In today's digital age, networking goes beyond in-person events. Platforms like LinkedIn are powerful tools for building your personal brand and showcasing your expertise. Regularly updating your profile, sharing relevant content, and engaging with industry thought leaders can increase your visibility and open up new opportunities.

Online communities, such as industry-specific forums or social media groups, allow you to expand your network and connect with people beyond your immediate circle. Active participation in these spaces can lead to collaborations and new connections that might not be possible offline.

Building a digital presence that aligns with your career goals is crucial. Share insights, engage with relevant content, and be mindful of the image you project online. A consistent and authentic digital presence can boost your credibility and support your long-term career aspirations. Keep in mind that you also need to remain productive, so don't get lost or distracted in the social aspect and avoid doom scrolling at all costs.

Section 3: Seizing Opportunities for Career Growth

Positioning Yourself for Promotions

To position yourself for promotions, demonstrating leadership and initiative is key. Even if you're not in a formal leadership role, look for ways to take charge of projects or support your team by problem-solving and offering solutions. Showing that you can lead, even informally, signals that you're ready for more responsibility.

Going above and beyond in your current role sets you apart. Consistently delivering more than what's expected, whether by taking on additional tasks or improving processes, proves your commitment to the company's success and highlights your readiness for the next step. Focussing on quality, value, and service are possible starting points to show how you are different from your peers.

Equally important is communicating your desire for growth. Let your supervisors know that you're interested in advancing and discuss what specific steps you can take to get there. Being proactive about your career ambitions keeps you on their radar when new opportunities arise.

Being Open to New Roles and Challenges

Embracing new roles and challenges is vital for career growth. One effective way to do this is by seeking out stretch assignments that push you beyond your comfort zone. These assignments allow you to develop new skills and demonstrate your capability to handle increased responsibility. When you actively pursue opportunities that stretch your abilities, you not only learn but also show your commitment to professional development.

Volunteering for cross-functional projects can significantly expand your visibility within the organization. By working with different teams, you gain insights into various aspects of the business, build relationships across departments, and enhance your reputation as a collaborative and adaptable employee. This exposure can lead to new opportunities and pave the way for future advancement.

Additionally, be open to accepting lateral moves, which can provide valuable experience and insight that may not be available in your current role. While it may seem counterintuitive to move sideways, these positions can set you up for long-term advancement by broadening your skill set and network. Each new role you take on, whether upward or lateral, contributes

5

Chapter 4: Sustaining Long-Term Career and Personal Success

Section 1: Creating a Continuous Learning Mindset

Developing a Growth Mindset

Developing a growth mindset is essential for navigating the ups and downs of any career journey. It begins with viewing failures and challenges as valuable learning experiences rather than setbacks. Each misstep offers insight into areas for improvement, making it easier to refine your approach and build resilience. This shift in perspective allows you to confront obstacles with confidence, knowing that each experience adds to your growth.

Adaptability is another key component. In a world where industries and technologies evolve quickly, remaining open to change and willing to pivot is vital. By training yourself to adapt, you not only weather change but also find ways to turn it to your advantage. Embracing flexibility, whether in skill development or in redefining goals, ensures that you remain relevant and capable of responding effectively to new demands.

Finally, cultivate curiosity and a passion for lifelong learning so that you will sustain this discipline throughout your career. Seek out new knowledge through books, online courses, and discussions with experts. Consider creating a "Mastermind Group". A habit of continuous learning not only keeps your skills sharp but also deepens your understanding of the broader industry landscape. This proactive curiosity keeps you engaged and positions you to seize emerging opportunities, making the path of career growth both fulfilling and dynamic.

Staying Current with Industry Trends

Keeping up with industry trends is a cornerstone of career longevity and relevance. Engaging in regular professional development helps you stay on top of shifts in your field and builds a skill set that meets current demands. From online courses to workshops, choosing learning paths that align with your career goals can ensure your knowledge remains current and directly applicable.

Attending industry conferences and seminars is another invaluable approach, offering firsthand exposure to emerging trends and innovations. These events allow you to hear directly from thought leaders, participate in discussions on best practices, and network with like-minded professionals. If attending in person isn't feasible, many conferences offer virtual access to sessions, which can be just as informative.

Mentorship, including reverse mentoring, is also a powerful tool for staying current. Traditional mentorship connects you with someone more experienced who can guide you through complex industry landscapes, offering insights you may not find elsewhere. Reverse mentoring, where junior professionals share new trends or technological insights with more seasoned colleagues, can help you tap into fresh perspectives and younger generational trends. Together, these relationships not only keep your knowledge base dynamic but also enhance your adaptability in an ever-evolving professional world.

Setting New Challenges

Setting new challenges for yourself is essential to continual growth and progress in your career. By consistently pushing your limits, you give yourself the chance to reach new heights, which can build confidence and open doors you hadn't previously considered. This doesn't mean taking on impossible tasks but rather finding meaningful ways to stretch beyond what feels comfortable. Furthermore, new challenges can be related to physical exercise and hobbies which can assist with mental acuity. Consider getting outdoors and hiking.

Actively seeking out learning opportunities is another powerful strategy to expand your horizons. Whether it's enrolling in a new course, joining a professional group, or working with a mentor, learning with purpose helps you stay adaptable and versatile. It's also a way to meet others who are focused on growth, which can inspire and motivate you even further.

Embracing discomfort is often a sign that you're on the right track. When you feel nervous about a new responsibility or uncertain about stepping into a role that stretches your skill set, remember that growth often happens outside of your comfort zone. Over time, these challenges make you more resilient and capable, equipping you with a mindset and skill set that can handle whatever comes next in your career.

Section 2: Maintaining Work-Life Integration

Redefining Work-Life Balance

Redefining work-life balance starts with understanding it as a dynamic state rather than a fixed line to hold. Achieving balance often means adjusting your focus as personal and professional needs shift, allowing flexibility to play a central role. Some days, work may require more of you, while on others, personal priorities will take the lead—and that's a healthy approach when it's intentional and manageable.

Incorporating personal values into your work life helps create a more cohesive and satisfying experience. Aligning your actions at work with what truly matters to you, whether it's integrity, creativity, or helping others, makes your career feel more meaningful and genuine. This isn't just about the job you do but about how you show up to it, setting boundaries and choosing projects that reflect your core beliefs.

To create synergy between your career and personal life, look for overlaps that serve both. Consider your work goals alongside personal ones to see where they might complement rather than compete with each other. Building a career that energizes rather than drains you, setting aside time for both achievement and enjoyment, and creating routines that support your whole self can lead to a balanced life that feels both rewarding and sustainable.

Prioritizing Health and Well-Being

Prioritizing health and well-being is essential to career success and personal satisfaction. Physical and mental health form the core of your ability to perform, make sound decisions, and sustain long-term growth. When you're healthy, you're more resilient to stress, better able to focus, and more engaged at work and in life. People will enjoy your company more when you focus on and improve your health and well-being.

Mindfulness and self-care practices are especially valuable for professionals with packed schedules. Small, consistent practices—like deep breathing exercises, short meditation breaks, or a few minutes of stretching—can help you manage stress and stay present even during hectic days. Incorporating these moments of calm into your routine prevents burnout and gives you more control over your emotional and mental state. Consider an under the desk cycle!

To support a healthy work-life balance, build habits that promote wellness rather than sacrificing it. Regular exercise, a balanced diet, and adequate sleep set the stage for sustained energy and mental clarity. Simple, daily habits like setting boundaries on work hours, taking breaks to recharge, and engaging in activities you enjoy can lead to a healthier, more balanced approach to both work and life.

Avoiding Burnout and Sustaining Passion

Avoiding burnout and maintaining your passion for work requires early recognition of stress signs and proactive steps to regain balance. Burnout often starts subtly, with fatigue, irritability, or lack of focus. If you notice these, it's crucial to address them early by stepping back, reassessing your workload, or prioritizing tasks that align with your strengths and interests.

When motivation dips, recalibrating can help you rediscover your purpose. Reflect on your original career goals or the aspects of your job you once enjoyed. Sometimes a fresh perspective can restore enthusiasm, especially if you reconnect with what inspired you initially. Setting boundaries and making space for renewal, like vacations or mental health days, can keep your energy steady.

Passion projects are excellent for reigniting your drive. These could be initiatives within your role or side ventures that let you apply your skills creatively and reconnect with what excites you. Engaging in activities that feed your curiosity and align with your values can provide renewed energy and sustain your commitment in the long run.

Section 3: Leaving a Legacy

Becoming a Mentor and Leader

Becoming a mentor and leader is about using your knowledge to lift others, which in turn enriches your own career, personal growth, and spiritual well-being. Sharing your experiences and insights can have a profound impact on someone else's journey, helping them overcome hurdles faster and gain confidence in their abilities. This support not only benefits them but also deepens your understanding and mastery of your own skills.

Leadership isn't reserved for senior positions; it's about taking initiative and setting a positive example, no matter where you are in your career. Acting as a leader fosters a proactive mindset that inspires those around you and can create opportunities for collaboration, problem-solving, and innovation.

Mentorship benefits your development too, as it requires you to communicate clearly, adapt to different personalities, and think critically about your advice. This process reinforces your skills, strengthens empathy, and keeps you engaged in learning. Embracing mentorship and leadership enables you to contribute to others' success while building on your own strengths.

Giving Back to Your Community

Giving back to your community allows you to use your career success as a force for positive change, creating a meaningful impact beyond professional achievements. By identifying causes that resonate with your personal mission, you connect your career goals with something larger than yourself, enhancing both purpose and satisfaction. This alignment lets you channel your skills and resources effectively, whether through mentoring, volunteering, or supporting local initiatives.

Service is not only about helping others; it also deepens your own sense of fulfillment. Engaging in meaningful contributions strengthens empathy, builds networks, and fosters gratitude, all of which enrich your long-term happiness and success. Embracing community involvement adds dimension to your achievements, helping you grow both personally and professionally.

Sustaining Personal Growth Beyond Your Career

Sustaining personal growth beyond your career involves setting goals that extend beyond professional achievements. Consider what you want to accomplish in your personal life, such as developing new skills, enhancing your relationships, or contributing to your community. These goals can provide a broader sense of fulfillment and purpose that complements your career ambitions.

Finding fulfillment in personal projects and hobbies is crucial for a well-rounded life. Engage in activities that inspire you, whether it's painting, gardening, or learning a musical instrument. These pursuits not only provide joy but also foster creativity and resilience, which can positively impact your professional life.

Achieving balance between career, passion, and purpose requires regular reflection on your priorities. Allocate time for personal interests and ensure they are integrated into your daily routine. This holistic approach to growth enriches your life, prevents burnout, and enhances your overall sense of well-being, creating a foundation for sustained success in all areas.

6

Conclusion:

In conclusion, while navigating the complexities of a career can often feel overwhelming, especially during periods of struggle or stagnation, it is essential to remember that you possess the power to overcome these challenges and reshape your destiny. The journey may not always be straightforward, but with determination and a proactive mindset, you can create the future you envision for yourself.

Implementing SMART goals is a crucial step toward achieving both success and satisfaction. By defining your objectives in a specific, measurable, achievable, relevant, and time-bound manner, you lay the groundwork for focused and intentional growth. Coupled with self-reflection and thoughtful planning, this approach empowers you to take stock of where you are, where you want to be, and the steps needed to bridge that gap. Regularly reviewing your progress ensures you remain aligned with your aspirations, allowing you to adjust your course as necessary.

Ultimately, the most significant changes in your career and personal life originate from within. Your mindset holds immense power; it can either limit your potential or propel you toward extraordinary achievements. By taking charge of your thoughts and decisions, you can cultivate the resilience needed to navigate obstacles and manifest the change you seek. Embrace this power, and let it guide you toward a fulfilling and successful career that reflects your true potential. Remember, the journey is ongoing, and every step you take brings you closer to the life you desire.

Thank you

Thank you so much for purchasing and completing this book. Your commitment to your growth and success means the world to me. I hope you found valuable insights and inspiration to guide you on your journey.

If you enjoyed the book, I would be incredibly grateful if you could take a moment to leave a review on Amazon. Your feedback not only helps me improve but also assists others in finding the support they need.

Wishing you all the best as you continue to pursue your passions and create the life you envision. Peace be with you.

Warm regards,

Rick

7

Resources:

Brown, B. (2024, March 6). *How to Create a Personal Mission Statement That Guides Your Career Towards Success.* www.theladders.com. Retrieved October 25, 2024, from https://www.theladders.com/career-advice/how-to-create-a-personal-mission-statement-that-guides-your-career-towards-success

Calm Editorial Team. (2024, February 8). *7 deep breathing exercises to help you calm anxiety — Calm Blog.* Calm Blog. https://blog.calm.com/blog/breathing-exercises-for-anxiety

Coleman, K. (2024b, August 29). *How to write a personal mission Statement.* Ramsey Solutions. https://www.ramseysolutions.com/personal-growth/mission-statement-101#cookie-banner

Coleman, K. (2024, July 3). *What is burnout and how can you recover from it?* Ramsey Solutions. https://www.ramseysolutions.com/career-advice/avoid-burnout-at-work

Dalton, S. (n.d.). *The 2-Hour job search.* The 2-Hour Job Search. Retrieved October 23, 2024, from https://2hourjobsearch.com/

How to get Promoted — The Guide to Moving up. (n.d.). https://w

ww.linkedin.com/business/learning/blog/productivity-tips/how-to-get-promoted

Keiling, H. (2024, August 15). *SWOT Analysis Guide (With Steps to perform and Examples)*. www.indeed.com. Retrieved October 24, 2024, from https://www.indeed.com/career-advice/career-development/swot-analysis-guide

Lambert, B. (2024, October 15). *Why stagnation happens and how to move forward - GoodTherapy.org therapy blog*. GoodTherapy.org Therapy Blog. https://www.goodtherapy.org/blog/why-stagnation-happens-and-how-to-move-forward/

Leonard, K. (2024, July 9). *The ultimate guide to S.M.A.R.T. goals*. Forbes Advisor. https://www.forbes.com/advisor/business/smart-goals/

The Success Alliance. (2024, October 8). *What is a Mastermind Group? A Definition and tutorials • The Success Alliance*. https://www.thesuccessalliance.com/what-is-a-mastermind-group/

Weber, K. (2016, April 30). Rick Warren: Why God encourages Christians to "Fear Not" 365 times in the Bible. *The Christian Post*. https://www.christianpost.com/news/rick-warren-why-god-encourages-christians-to-fear-not-365-times-in-the-bible.html

What Does the Bible Say about Fear? (2020, June 19). Bible Study Tools. https://www.biblestudytools.com/bible-study/topical-studies/what-does-the-bible-say-about-fear.html

Working out boosts brain health. (2020, March 4). *https://www.apa.org*. https://www.apa.org/topics/exercise-fitness/stress#:~:text=Exposure%20to%20long-term

www.ingramcontent.com/pod-product-compliance
Lightning Source LLC
Chambersburg PA
CBHW070414230526
45471CB00006B/2807